Spoil

Spoil

Alyse Bensel

STEPHEN F. AUSTIN STATE UNIVERSITY PRESS

Production Manager: Kimberly Verhines
Book Design: Mallory LeCroy
Cover Art: José R. Vázquez

IBSN: 978-1-62288-273-1

For more information:
Stephen F. Austin State University Press
P.O. Box 13007 SFA Station
Nacogdoches, Texas 75962
sfapress@sfasu.edu
936-468-1078

Distributed by Texas A&M University Press Consortium
www.tamupress.com

Contents

ii.

Is it a lack of imagination that makes us come
to imagined places, not just stay at home?

Elizabeth Bishop, "Questions of Travel"

Spoil

i.

Three Days into Your Marriage

My gums bleed.
I lean over the sink
as I watch red and more
red dilute to pink. I fear
the bone is weeping
through tissue, like when
I was fourteen and under
anesthesia, the surgeon
failing to cover up
the wounds. I begged
my mother to peer into
my hurting mouth
with a flashlight.
She lied, *no bone here*,
until I could see it
for myself, white meant
to be hidden by flesh.
I believe in punishment
meted out by anyone but
my own body. I blame it on
the cake I've been eating
for meals. It's my wedding
so I'll shove it down
my throat. I don't wait
for an arbitrary year to pass.
I'll finish the last piece. Leave
it to me. There's no sin
I won't pretend to repent for.

There Are No Poisonous Snakes in Puerto Rico

In Kansas snakes take many forms:
> cottonmouth, copperhead, massasauga,
>> prairie, diamondback, timber.

I keep my distance from that extra pit between
> nostrils and mouths fitted for fangs, scaled rows
>> laid like a brick garden border.

The week before spring I walk by
> neighborhood children surrounding a medusa
>> head of mating plains garter snakes.

From my phone I read to the children
> about how these snakes do no harm.
>> The snakes, stubborn as cats, nap

beside car tires. I try to coax
> them away from the danger. My first
>> snake was a pencil-sized garter pissing

in my hand, making my skin slick enough
> to slip away. I know my fears are false.
>> There are no poisonous snakes where you are.

It's the pulse of animals that are all spine. I know that kind
> of exposure: with no venom, they are one
>> exposed muscle, sun-drunk and still.

The You I Loved

These are my darlings: a quick
bread that splits down the middle
during its final minutes in the oven,
the steamy prayer when I unmold a cake.
Some days I've done it right. Other days
I'm rebuilding each layer like a burning hot
jigsaw puzzle. Either way, I make it delicious.
Covering up my failures is what I do best.

I likened you to my favorite recipe
written by another woman. I thought I had
it memorized. But I left out cinnamon,
added too much flour, took the hot pan
out too early. The undercooked batter
was bitter in my mouth. She knew better.

Kitchen

I unzip fava beans and pop
them out of their thick shells,
separating what sustained
their growth, as my friend's son
chirps with his newfound voice.
I palm each fat comma.
I want to fill the world
with daughters who learn
how to braid, are mesmerized
by semiprecious stones. *Thank God
I had daughters*, my mother
repeated, until she didn't.
Beside the seeds that look ready
to burst, others arrive shriveled.
I labored for their flesh
in vain. All I have is promise.

Surrender

This forgetting is like singed air. Like furs gathering dust in the back of the closet. Like a tongue coated in honey. Like a palm pressed against a concrete floor. Like a whale song caught between floating ribs. Like peach pits soaking for almond liqueur. Like connective tissue's elastic softening. Like a play all in denouement. Like a labyrinth, like one-way streets, like grace notes. Like peeling a winter orange, remainders of tropical heat. Like a mouth fogging up the window with each exhale. Like hair that darkens a shade from late summer to mid-winter, skin flecking off like a birch tree from exposure. Like becoming someone else, decomposing to this symphony, a chorus of pebbled meteorites.

The Expanse of a Digital Coastline

I annotate meaning,
wring it out,

rework your letters
until they fit into a small

box of assorted chocolates,
coconut, maple, coffee

that dissolve on my tongue.
Sweet forgetting. This morning

I am adrift on an island
bent for tourists: bright

flowers, blue waves,
green anoles,

a sun setting brilliant
off the coastline.

I lie down with you
among pixelated ferns

as I focus on one
photograph at a time.

I resolve to capture
any reality. I make

the crocuses
dotting the lawn

unreal so I can grant
power to what I am

waiting for:
your answer.

Jealousy in the Hypothetical

In which I am bone china, my delicate cheeks chipping off peach paint.

In which my skin crawls with living tissue not my own. Red mites pour from my wounds.

In which I am an assortment of objects: Lego blocks, a glass cloche, collector stamps, upturned quartz.

In which I am the feared weevil in the sandbox. The girl who scrapes the freckles off her nose with sand. Those melanin dots whorl away like pill bugs.

In which we never cross the border.

In which I pray to a fern in the crook of an oak tree, its slick inner corners.

In which I am the woman. In which I was never the woman at all.

Instagram Feed

The aperture inks

radial lines. The sun
sets alongside
grazing cattle

on an infinite loop—

Crested anole.
Confetti. A fly rests

on coral fungus.
Raining gems,

golden glitter. Knife
and tile, hot days

for darkling beetles.
Those sunset limbs
stitch a knuckle

back together.
Resistant ink and thorns.
This eye is a beating

dandelion seed
after bloom.

A spiral into gelatin,
rainy anvil days.

Patience:
the tissue has not yet

scarred. A portrait
of dew sharpening

on stalactites.
A freshwater

nymph balances on fine brush
hairs, budding like a sea

anemone. Boot soles
peeling. Mazes. This hunt

for prey. The work
of recycling earth.
Axe and broken walls.

A green midge fly rests
on pale lavender petals.

Those loves
thin as stick insects,
blotches of light

behind them, all memory.

Facebook Messenger Pastoral

I say prairie. You say nowhere
                close enough to the ocean.
On your drive to work the sunlight

      glaring off the mountains
must be the same that filters
                through my Midwestern paned

windows. From my landlocked island
      I trace the Kaw's path, a thread
in the embroidery of rivers

                that feeds into the gulf. A salt
cure for distance. But I won't write to you
      about how last night a man at the bar

overheard me say your island's
                name in my mouth.
He summoned those mountains

      on his phone. El Yunque. Direct flights
are cheap, he reminded me. I choked
                on my pineapple vodka. All these

years are for nothing.
      I do not leave. You do not return.

Shotgun

Let's start with her, pregnant, you,
unknowing, then knowing, me,

learning. I'm tired of this narrative
I've numbed to, like a twelve-gauge

fired off too many times against
my shoulder. I used to watch

my father disassemble and clean
his guns, then put them back together.

My non-pregnancy is an anti-narrative.
The hollow in my throat

constricts as I'm written out.
People ask me why I know so much

about motherhood and childbirth.
They ask me how many children

I have. I reply, *none*. The narrative stops.
A wedding, an ultrasound,

a countdown to when you disappear.
I cease to matter. My potential

children don't exist. I met a woman
who married because, two months

into dating, she took antibiotics.
Her son was round and luminous.

She could not believe he existed.
We discussed caesareans,

mastitis, stitches, the slow
healing process. Postpartum.

She asked me to find
her husband. He ignored her.

The shotgun's primary parts:
the barrel most of all, where you

pull the snake through, scrub
the chokes, clean apparent filth

off the action. Who made
the weapon? Who harbored it?

I have the story out of order.
There are too many moving parts

I mistook for an opportunity
to clear this up. I keep on missing

everything you left out.
This narrative may not

hit its intended mark. I blame
any misfire on my ignorance.

Weigh Your Options

Reply, keep in chat, replay then disappear, glimpse your teenage self, an exchange fraying in the wires. Send. Hope to be seen, be read. A record of angles and filters, even unedited an artifice. Decode the floating dots, the voice clips, a language less and less familiar. Forget words. Fail to correct what could fill in those gaps.

Succumb to the grid that performs happiness. Wait behind the camera for the shutter to click, the aperture to close. Guess where you fail at attracting. An ibis wades through the marsh seeking out crustaceans. Grind that grit into your teeth. Picture yourself afloat, doubling back. Tap and tap the screen's mined parts refined and assembled from labor made invisible an ocean away.

Stalactites shine from a headlamp's light as you dangle above placid water. Burrow and lean into the half-dark cave, your memory of this patterned world carved into the grooves.

Macro/cosmos

Those plant fibers
could be skin

near shiver.
Gravity pulls

water into teardrops
toward the ground.

Through that tiny
flashing star

someone must be
there, looking in.

Your Newborn Son

was born into a difficult meter,
his world all syncopation. I hum
a countermelody across thousands
of miles, willing my body to metronome.
A chest rising and falling. Be sure, be still.
The doctors count every missed beat.
He is filling your score with navy ink,
in flux with the tides. I write new patterns
conducted in common time, banish
adagio. You unfurl the pages,
ready for a libretto I dare not learn.

Gardening

I began with another woman's garden
built on gravel: lilacs and daffodils,

the resurrection lilies shooting up
their single stalks for one dusty pink bloom

before they collapsed. I guessed where
her bulbs would spring up around my own.

I planted phlox over her phlox, mine
low and creeping, hers tall and greedy

for the sun. I let the tulip petals
collect in the yard, not wanting to lose

that wilting heaviness. I reversed
photosynthesis as I breathed in to take

instead of give. I dug up broken
terra cotta, pieced fragments back together.

I was bone china—all animal
ash once molded to translucence

by a woman's hands, now a splintered
accident she had long since forgotten.

Todo Cambia

We were once gods of muscle,
untouchable to everyone
we loved, most of all ourselves.
You held sweet orange
pulp in your mouth.
I stretched then collapsed into
my smallest shape,
every fold a jagged tick
mark on my hips.
You counted the years,
crumbling like a river valley
in drought bound
to catch fire. You set the fuse.
I struck the match.

Hurricane Season

Disaster has been brewing all spring,
its genesis slick as an overripe plum

that falls in a heap of skin and pulp.
Clouds gather like starlings. A widening mouth

borrows the ocean. Fast talker, yarn spinner,
spool thick with clouds. I'm safe in the middle

of the continent—no shoreline to trace,
no widow's walk to pace. I open windows

to welcome a wind that when caged
can collapse walls, level an island.

The news reports a surging tide,
a narrow miss. While the ocean ticks

up degrees, I read the weather
as a series of chances:

roll the dice, be ready to lose.
Houses are a game of pick-up sticks,

playthings built to collapse.
When there is no more tree line,

everything kneels. Tragedies
on the seismic scale don't even

register on the news. No one blames
this violence on themselves

but after, parents won't give
their children those names

for years, won't put destruction
in such a small body.

Grief—a Fiddlehead

unfurling. My head
bows to my chest.
My spine curves,
softens with steam
in the bath. I become
easier to digest
like stewed rhubarb.
I am that mild
cultivated poison.
My throat refuses
to burn. I'm more
pliable than I'd like
to think. I set
the house to boil.

24

Tourism

Be a tourist in your own home,
its skeletal walls flayed of plaster flesh.
You may wonder why each picture frame
seems empty. No one there is familiar,
so pass among their faces as if they were
silk curtains, luxurious but airy volumes.
It's insignificant, and yet you can't quite
understand the beauty of an abandoned silo
that incubates saplings in its hollow body,
where you promise but make no guarantees.
The scene is here for you, and only you,
and whoever else happens to search
for that country road on their phone.
Look at each room from every angle.
The house is no more than a wooden frame.
Now tour your own body. Anchor your toes—
the swaying catches everyone off guard.
Like your family home, the body's repairs
are not included. Busted pipes, faulty ankle,
worn roofing, a rupture. Don't let
the beating stop. Be like your favorite
porcelain clock: cry out the hour, spring
forward, turn back time with your hands.

Like Ritual

I hold your face in my hands,
pinching the screen to control

each frame. My search spans
years eclipsed into a decade

written in letters crossing a sea,
a continent, messages received

through the wires. I'm revising
our history in metal and plastic.

The hurricane marred
your vistas, wounds splattered

across the island. Landslides
and uprooted trees, erasures

on a horizon. The wind turbines
remain. A long and short view—

your camera settles on
a male anole who flares

his red dewlap at his rival
in the neighboring tree

to defend his territory. I name
and unname in captions,

adjusting brightness
and saturation, sharpening

focus, as I send my imperial self
from afar in likes and loves.

Auto-Translate Sonnet

See: Sky

See: The seams where you tore apart, mended in rivers

See: A thing living off tension

See: An orb weaver the size of a robin's egg, coiled in the center of her web

See: How a bruise pools to shadow

See: Proof of minor resurrection

See: Crushed tile

See: Another woman's freckles

See: Reflection

See: Up to your knees in a muddy stream

See: No translation

See: Names I'll never hear

See: The Anvil

See: Reactivate reactivate reactivate

Web

I pretended this field
submerged into ocean,

cut grass could regrow
into a meadow. When I

remembered your body,
you contained a forest.

My torso snapped rigid,
pursued girl turned tree.

Mossy teeth. I could have
been an orb weaver threading

a sanctuary torn by wind
or your carelessness.

I refused to solve
your labyrinths—

there was one way in,
one way out.

Directions

The first man who showed me
how to pump gas left his truck
engine running as he filled the tank.
He turned off the ignition, breathed
never do what I just did. I'm prone
to accidents in cars: the semi grazing
the passenger's side where I felt
the heat from metal friction.
My professor, surveying the damage,
looked past me. *One more inch.*
He shook his head while he cursed
invasive weeds. A blown tread
on the Florida interstate left me
sideways in the backseat, while a friend
was surrounded by a half-moon of knives.
From above highways look like humanity's
nervous system: arteries, pulsing with cars,
that feed into major and minor vessels.
I looked up the route from Mayagüez
to San Juan. It's not direct. It circles
around the edges—no clear way
through the middle or diagonal stretch,
no easy shortcuts to get from me to you.

Alternate Universe

I would live without hurt.
Wind turbines would crash
on grazing cattle or to the bottom
of the ocean. My hair would be brittle
as straw or damp with tropical heat.

None of these places would be mine.
I would stand on a coast, the sand
my children, forgiving when I crush their bodies,
rounded seismic miracles that endured
a relentless ocean until one day,
they, too, slipped away.

Anoles

I kept them in a terrarium
overgrown with ferns and nerve
plants and begonias, the humid
atmosphere's phosphorescent
sun sealed by glass and plastic,
pale imitation of a rainforest.
When I offered them crickets
coated in white vitamin powder,
brides thrown to quiet slaughter,
I observed the aftermath: mouths
like fine-toothed combs hinged
open wide, then in surprise when
I would find one nestled in a shoe
or scuttling around the kitchen floor.
My mother wished for their deaths.
We've made them too comfortable,
she hissed. *They'll live forever.*
Her slight green nightmares
were given a second chance.
The crickets trilled in the closet,
my loud and lonely forest.
I never took them out for fear
of tragedy mistaken for spectacle.

Neighbors

My neighbor slept while her half-feral dogs
escaped between the rotten fence slats.
When she woke up she carried a bag of kibble
to the sidewalk, shaking it and pleading
for them to return. The family at the end
of the block vanished, leaving the yard
littered with cans, barbeque tools, a broken
plastic bike, the skeleton of a baby
carriage. Disconnected satellites huddled
in the corner lot unable to search
for any signal. It was like that when
you disappeared—I kept hitting send
only to receive planetary silence.

Litany Broken by Praying Mantis

For the curated image, the sentence
       in replica hearts, the bots toiling
for the algorithmic science of affection
       that predicted the passing glance
suspended for years, a pause
       on the screen while we touch glass,
the illusion of flesh underneath
       high resolution in a self that mimics
gazing into each other's eyes,
       for the fantasy slipping through
the screen that obeys swipe and scroll
       when the icon illuminates,
conjecturing the body outside.
       For the winds surrounding
an island ruined by capital that consumes
       a need for rumors living in captions
meant to describe the image. For giving narrative
       to the same story. For pausing
at movement on the sidewalk. For the praying mantis
       who judges the inch gap between concrete
and grass, her head swiveling. For telling her
       to go back to her green world,
and we'll go to back to ours, obscured
       by all the digital colors
held in our ghostly and oh so real palms.

Vinegar and Honey

You are insect today,
flighty but easily seduced
with sugar. I drink wine
in bed, empty the litterbox,
anything a pregnant woman
should not do. I lace vinegar
with dish soap to cure all
the sweetness in my kitchen
and ward off fruit flies
drawn to rot. I dress
my unrepentant feast,
my mouth full of honey
that dilutes the spoiled wine
I held too long under my tongue.
Sundays, I am on my knees.
Evenings, I break my fast
with a meal that quiets
my sharp thirst. I scour
the house. I read your letters
empty as shed cicada skins,
a memory of the shiny nymph
that fled for its short ticking life.
Once I make a crown
from those exoskeletons
I know you will mistake
me for one of your own.
You will linger despite
the dangerous cold to cry
your dying tymbal song.

ii.

I Confess

I married a man who believed everything
I said. Couldn't he see the snakes
in my hair? The pomegranate seeds
I clenched in my teeth? He admitted
he didn't know how to open the fruit,
with its thick wax that kept those many
honeycombed wombs safe. I bit into red.

Instructions for Hunger

Give up peeling the unruly
mango skin from your teeth.

Send yourself to bed without supper.
Boil water but refuse the tea

you kept for years for a special
occasion you thought had arrived.

Suck on honeysuckle blossoms,
their fleeting sweetness enough

of this earth. The unopened jam
and blackberry shrub in the pantry

have soured from ants and mold.
A promise, a primrose, a poison

fruit soaked and plumped for molds
you fill with batter but never bake.

Fritillary

I was pretty but not too pretty.

I kept my head down, counting

sidewalk cracks, perpetually nodding.

Always agreeable. My *no* sighed

to *yes*. Easy to bend. The shock

when I emerged year after year,

trying to choose a direction

closer to the sun, following

any simulacrum of who I could be.

I shuddered off my petals.

I grew all stamen, all unfruitful sex.

Dear Distance

I'm a smaller woman   than I used to be
        smaller minded   too
and generous   with myself   pouring coffee
        licking banana bread batter
    staining my hands with graphite

                I cherish carbon-on-carbon
        action   the kind you'd like to see
shedding cells mixed
    with dust mites and pollen

my castoff life is
                leftovers I forget
    to slough off in the mornings
        I'm trying to   reabsorb the world

take on mass and give my flesh
        a thrill   from the inside out—
    those gaps where he's still there

digging in dirty   fingernails and all
        that suppleness attempting
    to push away and down

Lies to Tell the Body

I became the opposite of orgasm,
        breathing with the cyst
nestled in my left ovary, where the pelvic
        bone juts up to meet
skin and socket. I tongued demands,
        a steel countertop parallel
to my spine, while doctors insisted I could
        conduct animal electricity.
A spark would jolt my limbs
        to swagger off
the table, proof of something alive
        inside my muscle.
Could I keep the yolk whole, a tiny
        fluid-filled sac that *if it bursts,*
it bursts? It would have been a relief
        to lose a little more. *You could stand to lose*
more, he told me. Weighing pears, he estimated
        how much I would need, suggesting
serving sizes, his perfect portions.
        My uneaten bite,
my refusal to measure. I left one
        curled arugula leaf or crusts
from toast. The year of almost. The year
        of maybe. Men moved
their unsteady chins up and down.
        They told me, *if only*,
my body a tragedy. If I burst,
        I burst, no more hurt than
the sharp pinch from a man bumbling

across my feet. I watched
my tropical fish die from fin rot. The tetras
went first. My blue
gourami the last, half floating, half swimming
on the water's scummy edge.
Two red drops and two yellow drops to stop
the infection. It still
spread. I was never at home. I combed every aisle
of the grocery store, my nails
digging in for miracles. I harvested
tomatoes, chard, green beans.
I was not a morning person.
I was not a night
person. I was a midday creature that slept
opposite of any man.
I stayed awake longer. After that year, I grew
all muscle and sinew:
my husband looked at me like a panther. He cut
my haunches on his teeth,
pressing the mechanism inside my pelvic floor—
reincarnate, reincarnate.

Wound

Strung tight
and gristle
the stretch.
could easily
white-socked
I memorized
the steps. What
her hips to
in the machine
tinny music.
a song of pins
to life painted
Tongue like a
and broke
beyond repair.

like a fiddle
I was unable
The other girls
curl their pinkies
feet. Not much
choreography
bends when
gravity? Automatic
tracking an infinite
To be unspooled
and steel combs.
face unchanging.
damselfly I snapped
a spring-loaded

hamstring
to glide into
in gym class
around cuffed
of a dancer
numbly repeating
a girl surrenders
ballerina trapped
circle wobbling to
from the crank
Stiff-limbed I sprung
Too tight. Too bad.
up and out
creature

Self Portrait as Mermaid Midge Barbie™

My elbows are unable to bend, shoulders over
rotated. Dislocated. As Barbie's third-closest friend

I couldn't cut the rebranding. I compared waists:
mine a little thicker. A tight-lipped smile. Perpetually

holding my breath. Apply too much pressure
and my arms snap right off. But I'm still more sturdy

than porcelain dolls. Here's the difference: you can
find me in the trash with my cheeks in one piece,

my jeweled hair, tinged chlorine green,
smudged with gum. A midge fly, a beauty queen.

All I know is that there is a body. I must be moved
to act. My drowning is in hypotheticals.

The girl knows the motive. I know the murder.

Catch and Release

Near the trail we found the spring.
In its shallows two rainbow trout,
recently released, circled one another,
a push and pull, like two magnets

attracted to their polar opposite
forces. The trout moved slowly
as if they were still inside the hatchery
up the road where I paid a quarter

to feed thousands that writhed
like eels in their holding pens.
It was trout all the way down
replenishing the streams

every morning, their excessive bounty
so different from the indoor pool
made for timed fishing at the outdoor
show: I tried to catch the palomino,

a pale flicker in the water, luring
it with an artificial neon flame bait
nestled at the end of a rented hook.
The trout didn't fall for the ruse.

At the hatchery they scrambled
for the pellets we threw to them,
their mouths small imperfect
exclamations. The young trout

began to lash out of their infinite loop,
dissolving their spell. I could have
jutted my fingers into the cold water
I was not meant to touch, driving them

upstream to end their hunger
on a fly fisherman's hook, becoming
what they had been born and raised
to do: be another's meal for sport.

Float Trip

That teenager in a Confederate flag bikini could be my new Disney princess of hate. She could conjure the waters into whirlpools. She could pop open rafts with rocks she turns blade sharp. She could hold that blood-red Jell-O shot like a cursed ruby, place it in her braided crown. She could quicken the current and not do much of anything else, maybe toss her Coors to the wind, blow me her rebel kiss.

Your Eye Is a Red Dwarf Planet

and the cornea a black hole
in reverse. The veins are rivers
coursing tissue continents.
A small sun near the surface
is trying to burst. When you sleep
that planet pulses, enveloped
by a dark atmosphere. I don't want
you to forget that in this metaphor
the planet, the eye, are dying.

Possum

for S and J

She had to give his phone
to her best friend, who found
not tit pics but the possum
on my porch, night's blank
slate behind it, eyeing cat food
left out for neighborhood strays.
I knew it was already gone.
I had found it on the road days
before. She kept the photo,
inscribing any meaning onto
whatever he left behind.
That goddamn possum
he thought worth saving,
that and the steer skull
stowed away as part of her
Christmas present. She told me
to keep any bones I found
so she could hang them
on the wall to keep the skull
company, the scavengers
having already left to continue
searching for what would
fill their insatiable desires.

Happy Accidents

I'd pay good money to watch you eat that peach
again, he said to me in a moan. The peach,

nearly overripe. Every time I fuck up the timing.
I'm sexy when stumbling around with fruit, a clumsy

acrobat in backward lace lingerie. Those men
no less hungry a decade later, trying to slake a thirst

no one told me about, discover scars I had forgotten.
At twelve I jumped off a rusty swing and sliced

a layer of skin on the back of my knee. I remember
the wound when my finger grazes the scar,

pain made knotty flesh. I'll let my body heal crooked.
I aspire to evidence without effort.

Do Not Consume Raw

At Target I browse the seasonal produce, eyeing
the warning label on the shrink-wrapped rhubarb.

I think about tearing open the package right there
and chewing the stalks, a cow with her favorite cud.

Those precautions signal the kind of rage
that ends with me screaming in my car. Sometimes

I let the man I'm seeing in there with the sound
to see if he'll stick around. But I have more

men lined up like I'm playing pinball and have
fifty cents handy for another silver ball.

I push the button for as many scoreless turns.
I poke holes in the plastic. I want the rhubarb

to decay faster, the game to continue. I'm tired
of trying to pause time. One of these days I'll stop

with the night cream, face masks, hemp lotions,
argan oil. I need exposure to speed up the inevitable.

Sit-Upon

We wove yesterday's news for comfort,
played kick-the-can ice cream that was still
cream by the end, were greedy for mountain
pies crammed with tomato sauce and melted
cheese from the campfire forge, resisted
scraping the rare water penny from under
stream rocks, while the boys grabbed
crayfish, boiled them, squeezed off the heads,
dared another girl to eat burnt marshmallows.
We red rovered, Bloody Mary-ed, woke up
with dewy eyelashes, sleeping beauties
no one would kiss. Thinking we were dessert,
we took care of our sweetness ourselves.

Portrait with Carrot

I sit on a picnic bench,
my chin on my palm,
clutching in my hand
the root I won't eat
unless its rounds are steamed
and buried in butter
and brown sugar. The carrots
in the garden were replaced
with things I liked better—
green beans and zucchini
left to overgrow, saturated
with thunderstorm water,
for a love of too-big things
that lose their taste.
I now buy my carrots thin
and purple, yellow, orange
with wild lace tops.
I impose a wild modesty
on what I eat, as though
it's a vitamin I can absorb
to grow smaller, disappear.

Carnivore

The husband's stomach roiled with salt-cured honey ham, brown sugar, oven-baked chicken breast, roast beef, medium rare, slices he requested thick then stacked high. She refused to wash off the dirt that clung to the lettuce. Her body bruised on the inside, tiny papercuts in her stomach. She scented the air with lavender, lemon seeds, earl grey tea, sachets of soap, incense, embarrassed by the lingering smell of meatloaf or pork chili, a stench she gleaned from her husband's skin. Her good housekeeping cleared the house of carnivores. She brewed her cleaning solutions with vinegar. Closing the curtains to obscure the robin's nest, where the mother bird offered her guts to her naked offspring, she cupped the acid in her palms. She pretended to drink.

Portrait at 16

No concrete in sight
because you hid the city,
refracting summer evening
sun so her half-lidded eyes
appear green, not blue.
What she is saying, tongue
curled back, half-lidded,
her gaze diagonal, I cannot
remember. She addresses
someone who is not you.

This was never about
the photograph. It was
about how you sent
myself to me ten years
later, our remainders
rationed among ourselves,
age beginning to show.
I cannot know her, or you,
a back turned to me
as I am mid-sentence,
ready to pick up where she,
breathless, left off.

Suburbia

Downy-legged girls with dirty fingernails and bare soles pricked by thorny weeds. Inside, the home pretends to be innocuous: plaid bedspread, wood shelves, muddied sneakers stacked beside the door. I sent you trees changing to yellow and blood red. You wanted more. You craved that color. Today, I started at the beads of sweat clinging to a pot of boiling water, thinking they were small glossy beetles. I figured outside had sheltered under the floorboards for winter, insect need looking for a way in. I never know who is still hungry or who has learned to remain full until the next lush season.

Thumb

The hammer hit my mother's thumb
and replaced *straight* with *curl*
and *jagged* and *thick* and something
she would hate. Her thumbnail grew
like a wave. I watched her curse
how nail polish pooled in its valleys.
I'm vain like her. I won't go near
anyone holding a hammer or lift
furniture for too long. I can't help
but think ruin happens inside—
my grandmother after church
on Easter Sunday. Blood pooled
in her brain and never left.
She had been fretting over
the altar flowers, the white lilies
on the cross. My left ovary
staged a rebellion. Time clicks
into place when something's wrong.
Too many transvaginal ultrasounds
and I've never been pregnant.
A jealous queen devouring
a princess heart, I'll cut out
my uterus to eat raw. No, I'll roast
then savor the meat on my tongue.

The World Is My Flower Garden

MoDOT Adopt-A-Highway Litter Cleanup

I'm common but more dandelion
than anything prickly. The trick is how

I'm torn apart to resurrect myself,
taproots grinding new holes

like an oil drill. I inherit the earth
by my own merit, glittery and diffused

in every patch of cultivated soil,
a land where John Deere roams

the country roads, loose dirt filled
with pin-headed seeds that settle

down anywhere, cover the highway.
The hardest part is the spring melt

and overnight frost, when
I'm likely to ruin myself, rotting away

in knee-deep mud until the sun
bakes the fields of mosaic stems

and broken glass into a pottery
that cracks open to cut bare feet

and careless fingers. Pick me up
and you may get a fistful of pain

or a bouquet fit for a dollhouse
make believe: the table, neatly set,

the flowers held within the scene,
preoccupied with wilting.

Welcome to

Where corn meets cattle meets field

Where Midwestern flatness gives way to Ozark rock

Where tractors bear signs for walnuts

      Stuffed in wooden crates by the roadside

Where the roads run parallel to the tracks

      Trains burdened with loads of coal

Where the metal sheet-roofed bar is named *Times Lost*

Where Skinner's Barbeque packs up and leaves until May

Where the state tried to seize land from a farmer

Who painted the Ten Commandments on his barn

      Over and over until the black paint peeled

And his children painted a single coat of whitewash after

      They took him away but the scrawled commandment

      Thou Shalt Not Steal is still visible from the highway

And the barn bears its many scars

Prizes of Mostly Air

Dead cicadas arrived
with the mail. I once stole
abandoned exoskeletons
off picnic tables, oak trees,
gathering them in my shirt
like a woman filling her apron
with apples. Their barbed legs
pinned back my hair.
I was an insect queen,
a dreamy pestilence.
In the kitchen I plucked out
spider crickets smaller
than the crescent
moon of my fingernail
from mixing bowls:
their spindled legs,
bodies awkward humps.
I steeped one in my tea
by accident, then threw
the boiled and plumped
torso into the sink. I swept up
all those lifeless forms.
I waited for more to arrive.

The Body in This Lifetime

Mother warned me, *don't lift too much weight*
because no one likes a woman with muscle

yoked around her shoulders stretching fabric,
another way for clothes to unflatter.

I was given an ultimatum: salvation in loss
or pseudoscience shame. When a friend confessed

she did not recognize me, I didn't mistake
her surprise as a compliment. A trajectory

brokered in pain, where I took every step
as a newly legged maiden in a cursed fairytale.

My wedding ring slipped off my fingers.
The doctors approved. The men looked

like they might pinch my flesh as if testing
a cut of beef. They didn't need permission

to see if I was bloody and rare, ready to eat.

Acknowledgments

I would like to extend my gratitude and thanks to the editors of the journals in which versions of the following poems appeared:

The Adroit Journal: "There Are No Poisonous Snakes in Puerto Rico"
Bear Review: "Tourism"
The Boiler: "Dear Distance," "Do Not Consume Raw"
The Collapsar: "Auto-Translate Sonnet," "Possum"
elsewhere: "Suburbia"
The Fem: "Shotgun"
The Fourth River: "The Body in This Lifetime"
Glass: A Journal of Poetry: "Your Eye Is a Red Dwarf Planet"
Moon City Review: "Sit-Upon"
New South: "Thumb"
Plane Tree: "Anoles," "Surrender"
Quarterly West: "Three Days into Your Marriage"
REAL: Regarding Arts and Letters: "Float Trip"
South Dakota Review: "Grief is a fiddlehead," "And the Expanse of a Digital Coastline"
Stirring: A Literary Collection: "Jealousy"
SWWIM: "Self Portrait as Mermaid Midge Barbie"
Sycamore Review: "Hurricane Season"
Tinderbox Poetry Journal: "Fritillary," "Instructions for Hunger," "Kitchen"
Vending Machine Press: "Directions," "Happy Accidents," "Instagram Feed," "Lies to Tell the Body," "Prizes of Mostly Air," "Vinegar and Honey"

Portions of this manuscript were also published in the chapbook *Lies to Tell the Body* published by Seven Kitchens Press (2018).

My eternal gratitude to Adam Mills, who read many drafts of this collection, my family in Pennsylvania, and the East Lawrence and New York Street folks. Many thanks to the support of friends, colleagues, and advisors at the University of Kansas: Megan Kaminski, L. A. Wheeler, Kris Coffey, Callista Buchen, Sara Villanova, Simone Savannah, Amy Ash, Candice Wuehle, and Tim Lantz. Special thanks to Stephanie Johnson for envisioning a new order for this collection.

Thank you to the wonderful (un)motherhood panelists, Karen Craigo and Rhiannon Dickerson, with whom I read earlier drafts of this work at the 2017 C. D. Wright Women Writers Conference.

Thank you to Ron Mohring and Seven Kitchens Press for publishing some of this work in a gorgeous chapbook as part of the Summer Kitchens Series.

Many thanks to the 2019 Sewanee Writers' Conference, especially to Sara Henning, who has always championed my work, Elijah Burrell, Laura Murphy, Leona Sevick, and Emily Koehn, and workshop faculty Mary Jo Salter and B. H. Fairchild.

And thank you to José Vázquez, anole whisperer and photon wrangler, photographer extraordinaire, for the use of his images for this cover and his enduring friendship.

REBEKAH ALVIANI

ALYSE BENSEL is the author of *Rare Wondrous Things: A Poetic Biography of Maria Sibylla Merian* (Green Writers Press, 2020) and three chapbooks, including *Lies to Tell the Body* (Seven Kitchens Press, 2018). Originally born and raised in south-central Pennsylvania, she now lives in the North Carolina mountains, where she is an associate professor of English at Brevard College and directs the Looking Glass Rock Writers' Conference.

Printed in the USA
CPSIA information can be obtained
at www.ICGtesting.com
LVHW091500120924
790711LV00004B/17